The Life Cycle Of Babesia Bigemina, Smith And Kilbourne, Of Texas Cattle Fever In The Tick Margaropus Annulatus, Say

Emery Westervelt Dennis

THE LIFE-CYCLE OF
BABESIA BIGEMINA (SMITH AND KILBOURNE)
OF TEXAS CATTLE-FEVER IN THE TICK
MARGAROPUS ANNULATUS (SAY)

WITH NOTES ON THE EMBRYOLOGY OF MARGAROPUS

BY

EMERY WESTERVELT DENNIS

University of California Publications in Zoology

Volume 36, No. 11, pp. 263–298, plates 23–28, 1 figure in text

Issued January 20, 1932

University of California Press

Berkeley, California

————

Cambridge University Press

London, England

THE LIFE-CYCLE OF
BABESIA BIGEMINA (SMITH AND KILBOURNE)
OF TEXAS CATTLE-FEVER IN THE TICK
MARGAROPUS ANNULATUS (SAY)

WITH NOTES ON THE EMBRYOLOGY OF MARGAROPUS

BY

EMERY WESTERVELT DENNIS

INTRODUCTION

The members of the sub-order Piroplasmidea are protozoa that parasitize the red blood corpuscles of mammals, but do not form the pigment that is characteristic of the malarial parasites *Haemoproteus* and *Plasmodium*. They are simple in structure, consisting essentially of a small bit of cytoplasm and a nucleus. The larger forms frequently have a punctiform granule or blepharoplast that is connected to the nucleus by a chromophile fibril or rhizoplast. The piroplasms are typically pear-shaped with the nucleus situated toward the broader end of the parasite (pl. 24, fig. 7).

The sub-order Piroplasmidea is represented by two families, the family Babesiidae Poche (1913) and the family Theileriidae Poche (1913). Members of the family Babesiidae multiply asexually within the erythrocytes of their mammalian host by division into two or more, rarely four daughter individuals, while the members of the family Theileriidae reproduce, also asexually, by a definite process of schizogony within the endothelial cells of the internal organs.

Each family is composed of but a single well defined genus. The genera *Babesia* Starcovici (1893) and *Theileria* Bettencourt, França and Borges (1907) constitute the families Babesiidae and Theileriidae respectively. This paper deals primarily with the largest of the three species of *Babesia* found in cattle, *Babesia bigemina* (Smith and Kilbourne, 1893).

The first observations on the piroplasms were those of Babes (1888) who observed the parasites in the blood of Roumanian cattle which were suffering from haemoglobinuric fever. This observer, however, failed to recognize the protozoan nature of the organism. He named it *Haematococcus bovis,* and believed that he had cultured it *in vitro.* Five years later Smith and Kilbourne (1893) published the results of their epochal work on *Babesia bigemina* in which they not only recognized the true animal affiliations of the parasite, but demonstrated that the disease was transmitted in nature only by the bites of certain ticks. This was the first demonstrated instance of an arthropod serving as a biological vector of protozoan disease.

Smith and Kilbourne named the parasite that they found in the blood of cattle in the southern part of the United States *Pyrosoma bigeminum.* In the same year Starcovici (1893) reviewed Babes' work and named the parasite observed in Europe *Babesia bovis.* He found that *Pyrosoma* had been used as the generic name for an ascidian, and hence was not available, so that Starcovici's name *Babesia* is the valid one. The name *Piroplasma* was suggested by Patton (1895) and has been widely, although incorrectly, used.

The development and life-history of *Babesia bigemina* takes place in two hosts. The parasite reproduces asexually in the red blood cells of the bovine host by binary fission (Smith and Kilbourne, 1893; Nuttall and Graham-Smith [as *B. bovis*], 1908; Dennis, 1930) following a simple sexual cycle in the tick that effects the dissemination of the disease.

Binary fission is inaugurated by duplication of the blepharoplast and rhizoplast which then push out into a pair of symmetrical peripheral lobes of cytoplasm (pl. 24, fig. 8). The lobes grow at the expense of the parent, and fission is completed by division of the nucleus and separation of the two daughters. The two parasites then rupture the host erythrocyte and are free in the blood stream for a short time before entering other corpuscles. The destruction of the red blood corpuscles in large numbers gives rise to the symptoms and pathological manifestations of the disease. In acute cases so much haemoglobin is released by the rupture of the erythrocytes that the urine is red, giving rise to the colloquial name of "red-water fever" for the disease.

It is the purpose of this paper to trace *B. bigemina* through the tick and to describe the various developmental phases. Koch (1906) observed certain "club-shaped bodies" with radiating processes in the gut of ticks which had fed upon blood infected with *B. bigemina.* Dschunkowsky and Luhs (1909) observed similar forms of *B. motasi.* The nature and relationship of most of these forms, however, are still obscure. Crawley (1915) reported finding numerous club-shaped bodies which he described as ''gregarinoids'' in the ova of *Margaropus annulatus,* which were presumably infected with *B. bigemina.*

The most complete and accurate observations previously published about the development of *Babesia* in the tick are those of Christophers (1907) who made a study of the life-cycle of *B. canis.* Many points in this work were not clear, however, and Christophers' conclusions have not been widely accepted.

Smith and Kilbourne (1893) demonstrated conclusively that *Babesia bigemina* is transmitted from host to host only through the agency of *offspring* of female ticks which had previously fed upon the blood of cattle which, at the time of feeding, were suffering from, or had recovered from an attack of Texas fever. The obligatory vector of this protozoan parasite in North America is the American cattle tick, *Margaropus annulatus* (Say), and the life-history of *Margaropus,* a one-host tick, makes the life-history of *Babesia* inseparable from the developmental cycle of the tick. For this reason it will be necessary to present certain details of its anatomy and embryological development before discussing the developmental phases of *Babesia.*

ACKNOWLEDGMENTS

The writer wishes to acknowledge his deep appreciation of the helpful advice and suggestions of Professor C. A. Kofoid, under whose supervision this investigation was conducted, and his very great indebtedness to Dr. Charles W. Rees, of the Iberia Livestock Experiment Farm, Jeanerette, La., whose kindness and generosity in supplying ticks of demonstrated infectivity and known history made much of the investigation possible. The author also wishes to thank Dr. H. C. Hisel, and Mr. T. W. Cole for their cooperation in securing ticks.

MATERIAL AND METHODS

The ticks used in this investigation were utilized in two ways, namely for a preliminary study of the anatomy, embryology, and life-history of *Margaropus annulatus,* and for studying the life-cycle of *Babesia bigemina* in this tick, its definitive host. The ticks were procured from five sources.

(a) Several hundred specimens of *M. annulatus,* including all stages in the life-history of the tick, were procured from Dallas, Texas, through the efforts of Dr. H. C. Hisel, State Veterinarian for Oklahoma. These ticks were removed from cattle which were believed to be carriers of Texas fever and were used in studying the morphology and life-history of the tick.

(b) A large collection of *M. annulatus* was very kindly supplied by Mr. T. W. Cole, Inspector in Charge of Tick Eradication, Jacksonville, Florida. A communication from Mr. Cole states:

These ticks were collected from dairy cattle near Jacksonville, Florida, which we have every reason to believe harbor the micro-organisms of Southern, Splenetic, or Texas Fever.

(c) A large number of *M. annulatus* was collected by the writer during the summer of 1929 from dairy cattle just east of Texarkana, Arkansas, where Texas fever was endemic at that time.

(d) A fourth supply of fever ticks was collected by the writer in the vicinities of Abbeville and Delcambre, Louisiana, from cattle harboring *Babesia.*

(e) The ticks used in tracing the development of *B. bigemina* under controlled conditions were procured through the generosity and kindness of Dr. C. W. Rees, of the Bureau of Animal Industries, United States Department of Agriculture, in charge of the Zoology Division, Iberia Livestock Experiment Farm, Jeanerette, Louisiana.

The development of *Babesia bigemina* as reported here was observed in a series of ticks of known history and demonstrated infectivity. This series will hereafter be referred to as Series A. A second group of ticks, also of known history, but proved to be *non-infective,* were studied to determine normal appearances, and served as controls. The control series will be called Series B.

Series A was obtained in the following manner: A number of adult female *M. annulatus* was removed from a steer that was suffering from an infection of *B. bigemina,* the diagnosis of which was based upon microscopical examination of the steer's blood. It was demonstrated experimentally that these ticks had become infected by placing larvae, which were hatched from eggs laid by some of these females, upon a clean, susceptible bull. This animal reacted positively on the fourteenth day after being infested with the larvae. Both the ova and offspring of these infected females are included in Series A.

Series A was treated as follows:

(*a*) A small incision was made in the posterior lateral margin of the body of an engorged female tick. When such an opening is made in the wall of the body the turgid gut is immediately extruded for one or two millimeters. The exposed gut was washed thoroughly in sterile saline to remove any adhering guanin concretions from ruptured Malpighian tubules. A small incision was then made in the wall of the gut and smears of the exuded contents were prepared on slides or coverslips. This material was studied both in fresh smears in salt solution and in fixed and stained preparations.

(*b*) The incision in the body wall of the tick was extended around the entire body and the dorsal body wall carefully dissected free and turned forward so as to expose the viscera. The gut was then removed and the diverticula fixed for sectioning. The ovary and oviducts also were dissected out and fixed for sectioning. By these methods, both smears and sections of the organs involved in the early history of *Babesia* in the tick were obtained.

(*c*) It was desired to trace *Babesia* through the egg and into the larva of the tick. This was accomplished by isolating infected, gravid, female ticks in large test tubes which contained moist sand, and allowing them to oviposit for three or four days. The eggs were removed from the culture tube each day and placed in labeled tubes to be incubated. Incubation was carried on at 30° C. Some of these eggs were removed at regular intervals during the period of incubation and smears or squash preparations made; at the same time some of these eggs were fixed for sectioning. This method gave a series of preparations showing stages of development from the time of oviposition to the hatching of the hexapod tick larva, thus providing for the correlation of the stage in the cycle of *Babesia* with the stage of development of the tick.

Series B was obtained from female *M. annulatus* which had been reared upon a mule in order to clean them of *Babesia bigemina*. This series was proved to be clean of infection by rearing the ticks for two subsequent generations on susceptible steers without producing any symptoms of Texas fever. Series B was studied in the same manner as Series A in an effort to eliminate parasites not belonging in the life-cycle of *Babesia*. Microscopical examination of these ticks failed to show any *Babesia*.

Dissection.—In studying the anatomy of the adult tick, and in dissecting out organs to be fixed for sectioning, the tick was usually opened by taking it between the thumb and forefinger of one hand and making a lateral incision around the body. The tick was then placed in a shallow vessel containing salt solution and the viscera were exposed by holding the ventral part of the tick to the substrate with a needle and gently pulling the dorsal wall of the body free from the musculature by means of a pair of fine forceps. In some cases it was advantageous to partly imbed the tick in a mixture of paraffin and beeswax before beginning the dissection. Scalpels made of slivers of safety razor blades inserted in the end of a wooden needle handle proved to be very useful. The ticks were usually not killed before dissection.

Squash preparations were made by snipping through the anterior margin of the body wall of the tick, adult or larva, and gently squeezing the body between two slides. The slides were immediately placed in fixing fluid. This type of preparation proved to be much more useful in dealing with the larval stages than the smear, because the destruction of the tissues in it is much less than in the smear.

Fixation and staining.—Bouin's and Schaudinn's fluids, both used after warming to 30° C, were the most satisfactory fixatives. Smears which were to be stained with Giemsa were fixed either in alcoholic sublimate or acetone-free methyl alcohol. The Bouin-chloroform mixture suggested by Wenyon (1926, 2:1326) was useful in the fixation of ticks *in toto*.

Sections of tissues were stained with Heidenhain's iron-alum haematoxylin, Delafield's haematoxylin, or Ehrlich's acid haematoxylin. Erythrosin was used to advantage as a counterstain. Smears were stained with iron-haematoxylin, Delafield's or Giemsa. Giemsa's stain was useful in correlating observations with those of Christophers (1907) and others who used Romanowsky stains almost exclusively.

Clearing and imbedding.—Oil of cedarwood was the most useful medium used for clearing tick tissues. Xylol and chloroform were useful in clearing ova which were to be sectioned. Tick ova were very difficult to section and the results were never very satisfactory, although little difficulty was experienced in sectioning the ova in the ovary and oviduct.

Imbedding proved to be a very important factor in attempts to section ticks and ova. For sectioning the gut and ovary, parawax was a very satisfactory paraffin. For sectioning ticks and ova it was necessary to use paraffin with a melting point of 68–70° C, and to cut the sections at eight microns. Infiltrating *in vacuo,* and then under very slight pressure for a few minutes was helpful in working with nymphs and adult ticks.

THE LIFE-HISTORY OF MAGAROPUS ANNULATUS

The pioneer work upon the life-history and biology of the cattle tick was carried out by Cooper Curtice (1891, 1892), and a fairly complete summary with additional details has been presented by Hunter and Hooker (1907), and by Cotton (1908). The outline here summarized is taken from data given by these authors.

The life-history of *Margaropus annulatus* may be divided into two distinct phases, a parasitic period during which the tick is attached to its host, and a non-parasitic period during which the tick is at no time attached and during which it does not feed. The parasitic period begins with attachment and ends when the mature tick drops from the host and seeks a protected site on the ground for oviposition. After the tick has left its host there is a pre-oviposition period ranging from three days in summer to as many as twenty-eight days in winter. Oviposition usually begins about seventy-two hours after the tick drops from its host, and continues for eight or nine days.

The average number of eggs laid by a single female is about three thousand. The eggs are generally elliptical in shape but may vary because of pressure. The average size of the eggs is about 0.54 by 0.42 mm. (Hunter and Hooker, 1907), and they range in color from a yellowish to a deep brown. The average period of incubation is about thirty days, according to the temperature and the amount of moisture. The seed ticks that emerge from the eggs are minute hexapod creatures which become very active and move up onto a blade of grass or the highest available object, where they bunch in masses of a thousand or more and await the coming of a host animal.

The parasitic period begins when a suitable host animal brushes against the perch of the bunched seed ticks and they transfer themselves to it. If it is a suitable host they will attach themselves and will begin to feed about two days later. The feeding continues for seven to twelve days and the seed tick molt *on* the host. The result of the first molt is the eight-legged, slaty-gray nymph. The nymphs feed from five to twelve days, then molt once again *on* the host to produce the sexually mature males and females which soon mate and continue to feed on the host from four to fourteen days; when engorged, the adult females drop to the ground. It has been our experience that oviposition begins almost exactly seventy-two hours later. *Margaropus annulatus* is thus capable of completing its life-cycle in about sixty days, making three generations a year possible under the limitations established by temperature.

THE ANATOMY OF THE TICK

The internal morphology of *Margaropus annulatus* has been worked out by Williams (1905) and more completely and accurately by Allen (1905), hence a detailed description would be out of place here. As the alimentary tract, reproductive system, and salivary glands are involved in the life-history of *B. bigemina,* the structure of these organs must be considered in sufficient detail to enable us to correlate the life-cycle of *Babesia* with the organs in which it occurs. As our observations coincide with the descriptions given by Allen, his paper may be referred to for further details.

The *alimentary tract* of the tick is complicated in appearance, but rather simple in structure (fig. A, *1*). It consists of a median canal beginning at the mouth and ending posteriorly in an intestine that is without a lumen, forming a blind sac from which two lateral and one posterior diverticula arise. Beginning with the opening of the mouth, the oesophagus goes almost directly posteriorly, then turns sharply toward the antero-ventral part of the body, only to curve abruptly backward and upward to pass through the brain in about the median line (pl. 23, fig. 6). This course may be more direct in some specimens. After it passes through the brain, the tract extends posteriorly giving off opposed right and left branches. Almost immediately the main line runs ventrally to the cloaca as a blind lumenless intestine; a single branch, the posterior diverticulum, extends posteriorly as originally in the median line. Each of the right and left branches give rise immediately to five finger-like diverticula, the most anterior of which is the longest. The single posterior diverticulum gives rise to

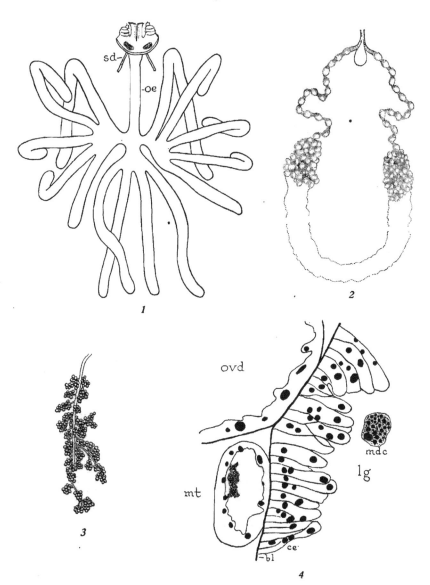

Fig. A. (*1*) A semidiagrammatic drawing of the digestive tract of *Margaropus annulatus*, dorsal view, showing lateral and posterior diverticula, × 5. (*2*) Semi-diagrammatic drawing of the reproductive system of a female *M. annulatus*, show-ing the single ovary connecting the two convoluted oviducts that terminate at the anterior ovipositor. The seminal receptacle is the anterior flask-shaped structure, × 5. (*3*) A single salivary gland, redrawn from Allen, × 20. (*4*) A camera lucida drawing of a portion of a transverse section of an unengorged female *M. annula-tus*, showing the nature of the wall of the gut, and the intimate relationship of the gut and the reproductive organs, × 150.

bl., basal layer; *ce.*, columnar epithelium; *lg.*, lumen of gut; *mdc.*, macrophage digestive cell; *mt.*, Malpighian tubule; *oe.*, oesophagus; *ovd.*, oviduct; *sd.*, sali-vary duct.

four similar branches. Thus there are seven blind branches of the gut on each side of the median line. These caeca are long, extending first peripherally, then ventrally, and finally median again. They branch again in minor secondary pouches due to expansion of the wall of the gut into all available spaces between the muscles and the reproductive system.

In the engorged gravid female the diverticula of the gut and the tubular organs of the viscera are almost inextricably tangled together. This fact is significant because of the large amount of surface of the digestive tract which is brought into intimate contact with the organs of the reproductive system into which it is necessary for *Babesia bigemina* to enter in order that its life-cycle may be successfully completed (see fig. A, *4*).

The histology of the gut is likewise important in its relation to the behavior of *Babesia*. The wall of the gut is composed of two layers, both thin, and when the gut is distended the thickness is so reduced that the passage through it by a parasite could be accomplished with great ease. There is an outer cellular layer, serving as a basement layer, that is rarely over five microns thick and is usually thinner. The other layer is an inner columnar cell layer, composed of somewhat amoeboid, club-shaped cells that extend into the lumen of the gut as single-celled villi, and is about thirty microns in thickness. In the lumen of the gut there are large amoeboid macrophage digestive cells, filled with red blood cells of the bovine host in various stages of digestion, and with dark chromophile masses which resemble the amorphous chromatoidal masses seen in *Endamoeba gingivalis*. The cells of the wall of the gut are secretory and have large granular nuclei. The columnar epithelium is a very loose structure so that the basal layer is essentially the only part of the wall of the gut which a parasite would have to penetrate (fig. A, *4*) in order to enter the reproductive organs.

The *female reproductive system* (fig. A, *2*).—The only external opening of the reproductive system of the female is the anteriorly situated ovipositor. The ovipositor opens internally into a relatively large cavity, the seminal receptacle, into which there also open two long, bilateral, convoluted tubes which are about 17 mm. in length. These tubes, the oviducts, are connected posteriorly by the single convoluted ovary, thus forming a complete loop that is very long. This system is wound in and out among the diverticula of the gut so that some part of it is in close contact with or very close to some branch of the gut at almost all points. The fact that the parasites enter the eggs is apparently not a matter of a tropism or preference; there is essentially no other place to go!

The *salivary glands* (fig. A, *3*) are a pair of compound alveolar glands resembling an elongated cluster of grapes. They are somewhat over two millimeters in length, and in the unfed tick they occupy about a fifth of the volume of the body. The salivary ducts enter the floor of the buccal cavity. The salivary glands also become entangled with the anterior caeca of the gut and the reproductive system.

THE EMBRYOLOGY OF MARGAROPUS

The literature on the embryonic development of ticks is meager and textbooks give no information about the subject. Christophers (1906) in his study of ticks preliminary to his work on the life-cycle of *Babesia canis*, gave a three-page account of the structure of the ovum and the embryology of ticks, but the description is too generalized to be of much use. There are two papers which give adequate accounts of the development of ticks: Wagner (1894) did a splendid piece of pioneer work on *Ixodes calcaratus*, and Bonnet (1907) gave an excellent description of the embryology of *Hyalomma aegyptium*. Apparently the ixodid ticks differ from each other in their development only in minor details, for Bonnet states, in reference to Wagner's paper: "J'ai pu verifier les observations de cet auteur et mes recherches ont confirme entierement ses conclusions." Except for a few minor discrepancies, Bonnet's description holds for *Margaropus annulatus*.

The mature eggs of *M. annulatus* are about 450μ in length, and 420μ in breadth. The ovum consists mostly of spherules of yolk which are imbedded in cytoplasm that appears to be coarsely granular when stained with iron-haematoxylin. The germinal vesicle is located toward the future postero-ventral surface of the egg in an area of the cytosome that is free of yolk (pl. 23, fig. 1).

Fertilization of the egg takes place in the oviduct of the female tick when the egg is freed from its ovarian follicle. Segmentation is usually well under way by the time that oviposition takes place.

Segmentation is of the superficial type, and at first involves only the area of the egg in which the germinal vesicle was situated. As the result of mitotic divisions of nuclei in this region, there is formed a thin germinal disc. This germinal disc, as the blastoderm, extends its margins until the entire yolk mass is enclosed by a cellular layer which is one cell in thickness (pl. 23, fig. 2).

, The differentiation of the endoderm begins in the postero-ventral region where segmentation first began. Here proliferation of cells from the blastoderm results in the formation of a loosely aggregated mass of endodermal cells which soon extends anteriorly along the floor of the blastodermic vesicle as a narrow band or ridge of tissue (pl. 23, figs. 2, 3, 4). The process of endoderm formation in the tick was considered as a process of gastrulation by Bonnet, who suggested that the region in which the formation of endoderm begins is comparable with the region of the blastopore in higher forms. In the earlier stages of endoderm formation, nuclei are to be found which have migrated deeper into the yolk mass; these are the endo-vitelline cells of Bonnet. Bonnet described the endoderm as being formed by the migration of these endo-vitelline cells to the periphery, but the writer has seen no evidence that cells migrate deep into the yolk and then *return* to the periphery to form tissue.

As in *Hyalomma*, the formation of mesoderm takes place as a proliferation of the ectental line on both sides of the endodermal ridge. These cells then migrate medially between the ectoderm and the endodermal band, and the mesodermal tissue grows anteriorly and dorsolaterally.

While the endoderm and mesoderm are being defined, proliferation of the ectoderm of the embryonic disc continues until it forms a relatively thick anterior plate that extends to the dorsal surface, and a similar but less extensive plate posteriorly as a caudal lobe (pl. 23, figs. 2, 3). At the same time a thin non-cellular cuticle, which is the outer body covering of the embryo and larva, appears outside of the peripheral blastoderm.

The anlagen of the appendages appear very early as six pairs of lateral buds of mesodermal tissue with a thin ectodermal covering (pl. 23, fig. 4). The two anterior pairs are situated toward the median line and form the mouthparts. The other four pairs are limb buds, but the most posterior pair is quickly resorbed to a small compact mass of tissue that gives rise to the fourth pair of limbs at the first larval ecdysis.

With the appearance of the limb buds, development becomes centered in the anterior end. The greater part of the anterior ectodermal plate forms the large ventral cervical ganglion or brain (pl. 23, figs. 5, 6). This body of cells acquires a lumen in the larger anterior mass, while according to Bonnet the smaller posterior portion which lies in the abdominal region gives rise to six pairs of ganglia.

The development of the endoderm is arrested for a considerable period of time following the completion of the primary endodermal ridge, while the other germ layers continue to develop with rapidity. The Malpighian tubes are about the first endodermal structures to appear. These structures appear as a pair of short tubes, one on each side of the midline in the postero-ventral part of the embryo. They can be seen quite clearly through the shell of the egg, and appear to arise directly from the yolk mass. As the Malpighian tubes grow they become filled with excretory concretions and appear as dark filaments. Short and rod-like at first, these tubes extend posteriorly, then dorsally, and finally anteriorly until each tube is shaped like the letter U with the base of the letter directed posteriorly. The excretory vesicle soon appears at the point of origin of the Malpighian tubes as a single chamber into which the tubes empty (pl. 23, fig. 6). An invagination of the ectoderm occurs at this point, and later breaks through forming an excretory orifice.

The buccal apparatus is formed concurrently with the appearance of the Malpighian tubes, from the first two pairs of appendages. The median first pair form the chelicerae, and the second pair form the palpi. The hypostome is formed by a ventral projection of the chitin of the body wall. The hypostome forms the floor of the buccal cavity, while the roof is formed chiefly by the appendages.

The salivary glands are formed postero-lateral and slightly ventral to the buccal apparatus from ectodermal cells of the larger anterior cell mass which are distinguishable by their larger size and the size of the nuclei (pl. 23, fig. 5).

The mesoderm goes chiefly to form the musculature of the tick. The earliest muscles to appear are the dorso-ventral muscles of the posterior region which arise by the muscle fibers penetrating the yolk and growing dorsally until they come in contact with the dorsal wall of the body. Since the endoderm does not appear for some time except in the anterior region, the appearance and arrangement of the muscles delimits the distribution of the endoderm and the pattern of the digestive caeca.

At the time of hatching, the external form and the appendages of the larva have been attained, the nervous system has reached its maximum development, the salivary glands and excretory organs are well developed, but the digestive system consists of little more than the buccal cavity, short pharynx, and the oesophagus, as the postero-dorsal two-thirds of the yolk mass has yet to be enclosed by the endoderm (pl. 23, fig. 6).

BABESIA BIGEMINA IN THE TICK

The sexual phenomena and sporogony of *Babesia bigemina* take place in the tick. The early phases in the developmental cycle occur in the lumen of the gut after ingestion of parasitized blood by the tick. The development of *Babesia* then proceeds particularly in the reproductive system where the ova of the tick are invaded and subsequently in the tissues of the embryonic stages of the tick.

The early stages of development were studied in fresh saline preparations, smears, and sections of the gut, but in no case were the parasites found in the gut in large numbers. Careful examination of the material, however, resulted in the detection of several forms of the parasite.

There were typical trophozoites which had recently been taken into the gut. These parasites were either free in the ingested mass, or incorporated in the wandering digestive macrophages or "liver" cells of the tick. Sometimes several occurred in a single macrophage. Parasites that are so phagocytized soon show signs of being digested. Pear-shaped and rounded forms of the parasite, mostly the latter, were observed (pl. 24, figs. 13 to 18).

In addition to the trophozoites in the gut, there are also present very characteristic forms which correspond to some of the "club-shaped bodies" described by Christophers (1907) as one of the early stages in the development of *Babesia canis* in the tick. These parasites (pl. 24, figs. 21, 25, 26; pl. 25, figs. 30 to 32) are the isogametes. There is also a form that is almost herpetomonad in appearance, but which shows no neuromotor structures, and stains very poorly (pl. 24, figs. 22, 23, 24). These parasites are probably degenerating.

The gametes are about 5.5–6.0μ in length, and have an appearance much like that of the vermicules of *Hepatozoon* in the mite (Miller, 1908) although they are frequently more flattened, or club-shaped. They arise simply by growth and slight modification of structure (pl. 24, figs. 19 and 20) from trophozoites that are indistinguishable from other trophozoites, rather than by the elaborate method described by Christophers (1907) for the origin of the "club-shaped bodies." The gametes could not be identified as to sex, all gametes being identical in appearance. These sexual forms are actively motile: when floating free in a fluid medium they undergo flexure from side to side, the more pointed end or "tail" being the more active: if attached to a substrate they show gregarine-like movement, proceeding with the blunt end foremost. As they progress, small protoplasmic processes best described as "papillae" are thrust out tentatively from the blunt anterior end.

When stained with iron-haematoxylin, the gametes show marked differences from the trophozoite-gametocyte. The cytoplasm is less homogenous, and the nucleus is larger and richer in chromatin. The chromophile extra-nuclear organelles, the blepharoplast and rhizoplast, are typically absent, but sometimes a well defined granule may be seen near the nucleus, and a fibril may be traced for a short distance toward the nucleus (pl. 24, figs. 25 and 26). The blunt anterior end usually stains more intensely than the rest of the cytoplasm.

Fertilization apparently takes place by the isogametes becoming associated first at the anterior end, as in *Hepatozoon* (Miller, 1908) and then fusing (pl. 24, figs. 21 to 24). The actual fusion of the gametes was not observed, and associated pairs are very scarce in the stained preparations; however, paired or associated gametes were observed in fresh smears of the gut contents in salt solution from six of the adult female ticks of Series A (pl. 25, fig. 32). These associated parasites were studied for lengthy periods but no further development was observed before they died or the preparation became too dry. Rounded bodies exhibiting two distinct nuclei (pl. 25, figs. 33 and 34), were present in stained preparations, and have been interpreted as later stages in syngamy.

Syngamy results in the formation of a motile zygote or oökinete which soon leaves the lumen of the gut. The oökinetes (pl. 25, figs. 35, 36, 37, 38, 40, 41, and 42) range from about 7.0 to 12.0 microns in length, and they are more characteristically club-shaped. The oökinetes usually show some structure at the anterior end. In the smaller, and probably younger forms, there is a small papilla-like structure (pl. 25, fig. 35). The larger individuals (pl. 25, figs. 38, 41)) have a cup-like crown which probably functions as a boring organ. This structure is lost shortly after the oökinete enters the egg of the tick (pl. 25, figs. 37, 40, and 42).

The oökinetes pass through the wall of the gut of the tick and into the contiguous organs of reproduction where they invade the ova. Usually only one or two oökinetes enter a single egg, but approximately fifty were observed in one instance. In our experience only the larger ova are entered.

In the ovum the oökinete forms a *sporont* (pl. 25, fig. 43). The sporont has a large vesicular nucleus, and forms a cyst wall about itself. The smallest sporont observed measured 7.5μ in diameter, and the largest one measured 12.0μ in diameter, exclusive of the wall of the cyst. The nucleus of the sporont or zygote divides (pl. 25, fig. 44) and there are formed within the cyst a number of *sporoblasts* (pl. 26, figs. 45 and 46).

The sporoblasts are somewhat amoeboid, many of them exhibiting fine radiating pseudopodia. The nuclei of the sporoblasts increase in numbers to form multinucleate amoeboid somatellas which migrate throughout the embryonic tissues of the developing tick. Because of their migratory activities we call the parasites *sporokinetes* (pl. 26, fig. 47) following the usage of Reichenow, 1921.

Owing to their amoeboid nature the sporokinetes are very pleomorphic. They may be round, asteroid, club-shaped, or drawn out into long tenuous forms as much as 15μ in length. The nuclei appear as well defined granules about 0.4μ in diameter, and range in number from four to about thirty-two. During the ontogeny of the tick the sporokinetes apparently form other sporokinetes by simple plasmotomy. Practically any tissue of the embryo of the tick may be infected. In many cases the cytoplasm of the host cell may be almost completely displaced by the parasites. Since much of the anterior embryonic cell mass is destined to become salivary tissue, some of the alveoli of the salivary glands come to be occupied by sporokinetes. As the period of incubation of the tick comes to a close, some of the sporokinetes undergo sporogony to form *sporozoites;* others may not form sporozoites until after the 'tick has hatched, as sporokinetes have been observed in the tissues of active larvae.

The sporozoites (pl. 26, fig. 49) are miniature trophozoites. They tend to be pyriform, have a characteristic nucleus, and the extranuclear granule or blepharoplast soon appears. The sporozoites are most numerous in the salivary glands and the connective tissue at the base of the limbs and surrounding the organs of the viscera. In some cases the contour of these small parasites gives the impression that they are dividing in much the same manner as does the trophozoite. The sporozoites are inoculated into the blood stream of the bovine host in the saliva of the feeding tick larva, and there set up an active infection of the red blood cells.

DISCUSSION

The only previous attempts to make a systematic study of the life-cycle of *Babesia* in the tick were those of Koch (1906) and Christophers (1907). Practically all other contributions to our knowledge of the subject have been random observations which were but incidental to the subject under consideration. The paucity of trustworthy observations is largely due to the fact that the economic importance of babesioses has centered interest upon biological control of *Babesia* by the eradication of the vector involved. Furthermore, the bewildering display of débris presented by a smear of the contents of the gut of a tick would immediately discourage anything less than a thoroughly conscientious attempt to find parasites therein. Also, when one considers that there are relatively few *developmental* forms of *Babesia* in the gut of the tick at any time and that the multiplication period of the parasite in the tick does not occur until near the close of its sexual cycle, it becomes more clear why the phases of development in the gut have been overlooked.

There is general agreement in the observations of Koch (1906), Christophers (1907), and those recorded above on the forms of *Babesia* present in the gut, but considerable discrepancy in interpretations. No investigator has been able to distinguish gametocytes from normal trophozoites of *Babesia,* and a false analogy of the life-cycle of *Babesia* with that of the malarial parasites has led to confusion.

Since nothing identifiable as a gametocyte has been found, it is agreed that the developmental forms of *Babesia* in the tick must arise from normal-appearing parasites which are freed in the gut. The isogametes arising from such normal-appearing forms were seen by both Koch and Christophers.

Koch (1906) observed that in the gut of *Rhipicephalus australis,* *R. evertsi,* and *Hyalomma aegyptium, B. bigemina* increased in size and produced long radiating pseudopodia or processes. These ''Stechapfelformen'' were observed associated in pairs, a phenomenon which Koch suggested was a kind of conjugation. The ray-like processes of the associated individuals were retracted and the two fused to form a globular body with two nuclei (*see* Koch, 1906, pl. 2, fig. 24). This globular form is undoubtedly the same as the one observed by us (pl. 25, figs. 33 and 34).

Christophers (1906*a*), in a preliminary note on the life-cycle of *B. canis,* reported a pairing of "club-shaped bodies" which gave rise to a rounded parasite exhibiting two nuclei and an achromatic line indicating the line of fusion. In his subsequent paper, however, Christophers (1907) reversed his conclusions, describing the formation of the club-shaped bodies by a very peculiar method of division of the larger rounded parasite. He does not state his reasons for the change in his interpretation, but the final paragraph of his description of the formation of the "club-shaped bodies" indicates that it was because he did not find the thing for which he was looking. Christophers (1907, p. 59) states:

> The method of development in the tick certainly suggests a sexual cycle, and it is immediately prior to the formation of the club-shaped bodies that one would expect the junction of the male and female elements to occur. As just stated, the double forms are not conjugation forms and the analogy of the development of piroplasma with that of the malarial parasite would lead one to suppose that the male element is small, and in such a situation as the gut of the tick likely to be easily overlooked. The absence of any definite observation regarding fertilization is not therefore sufficient at this stage to negative the view that the life cycle of development in the tick is a sexual one.

The only essential difference in the observations of Koch, Christophers, and the writer on the early forms of *Babesia* in the gut is relative to the ray-like processes of the "Stechapfelformen" described by Koch. Kleine (1906), Nuttall and Graham-Smith (1908*a*), Martini (1909), Knuth and Richters (1909), Thompson and Fantham (1913), and Ziemann (1913) have observed the formation of radiating pseudopodia in so-called "culture" forms of *Babesia*. The writer, however, is in agreement with Christophers (1907) in concluding that the formation of these ray-like processes is not essential in the development of *Babesia*. We have seen the production of very similar processes by *Trichomonas* from old cultures and in fresh smears which had become too dry, so that it seems probable that such processes are induced in *Babesia* by unfavorable culture media or by drying.

In previous work, the "club-shaped bodies" have dominated the life-cycle of *Babesia*. Koch (1906) saw certain club-shaped bodies in the ova of the tick, which were about four times the size of the trophozoites. Christophers observed club-shaped bodies in the gut, in the tissues of nymphs, and in the reproductive organs of adult female ticks. No distinction was made between the gametes and the oökinete, but Christophers did describe the formation of "zygotes" by the rounding up and growth of club-shaped bodies. In view of the fact that the so-called "club-shape" is characteristic of the oökinetes of the Haemosporidia, and that *B. bigemina* assumes a "club shape" several times in its life-cycle, the club shape should be considered as a consequence of the method of locomotion and tissue-penetrating activities of the micro-organism and has no special morphological significance as a "stage" in its sexual cycle.

The zygote of *B. bigemina* is present in three forms. It appears as the rounded body formed as the result of syngamy, as the active oökinete, and as the sporont in the ovum of the tick. Christophers described a "zygote" which was imbedded in the tissues of the gut and in the yolk of the egg. This "zygote" is considered to be homologous with the sporont of *B. bigemina*, although according to Christophers a cyst wall was never formed. The wall of the cyst of the sporont of *B. bigemina* was difficult to define in some cases, being indicated only by a sharp halo around the sporont, but it appeared distinctly in sectioned material stained with iron-haematoxylin (pl. 25, figs. 43 and 44). In some cases Christophers may have been dealing with young sporonts which had not yet produced the cyst, but his observations were made mostly on squash preparations stained with Giemsa and many of the "zygotes" figured by him look more like tissue cells than sporonts. Since there is no reason to expect marked differences between the individuals of *B. canis* and *B. bigemina* in corresponding stages of their life-cycle, it seems probable that some of the "zygotes" that Christophers was dealing with were artifacts.

The sporoblasts are but transitory forms in the life-cycle of *B. bigemina*. There is nothing outstanding about them except that they eventually give rise to the active sporokinetes which are responsible for the spreading of the parasite throughout the embryonic tissues of the tick. The formation of sporoblasts in the life-cycle of *B. canis* was described by Christophers, who included forms which were probably sporokinetes.

The sporokinetes are particularly important in the life-cycle of *B. bigemina* in the tick. They constitute the multiplicative phase of the life-cycle by means of which enormous numbers of the infective sporozoites are produced. Their migratory activities carry them into practically all parts of the body of the tick embryo so that it is certain that some of the salivary acini become infected. Since the sporo-kinetes are intra-cellular parasites, repeated cell division in the embryonic tissues undoubtedly aids in distributing them throughout the embryo. If it is borne in mind that the anterior ectodermal cell mass and the mesoderm are the most actively proliferating tissues of the tick embryo, it becomes clear why *Babesia* becomes concentrated in the salivary glands and the connective-tissue sheaths of the muscle bundles of the tick larva.

The sporozoites are the smallest as well as the most numerous forms of *B. bigemina* in the tick. In infected tick larvae some of the salivary acini become almost solid masses of *Babesia*. The sporozoites are most numerous in the loose mesenchyme cells which sheath the organs of the viscera; when they are especially numerous it is difficult to see the outlines of the parasites, but the more intensely staining nuclei of the sporozoites give the host cells the appearance of being filled with small chromophile granules. The sporozoites of *B. canis* were described by Christophers (1907), and Koch (1906) figures the sporozoites of *Babesia bigemina.*

RELATIONSHIPS

Babesia has long interested the protozoologist as well as the economic parasitologist. Whereas the latter has been primarily interested in the therapy and control of the diseases caused by the piroplasms, the former has sought to throw some light upon the relations of the Haemocytozoa to the flagellates.

Schaudinn (1904) pointed out the constancy of the apical chromo-phile granule in the trophozoites of *Babesia bigemina,* and suggested that this structure is homologous with the blepharoplast of the Flagellata. Breinl and Hindle (1908) described flagellated forms of *B. canis* from the blood of dogs, but subsequent investigation has failed to show the possession of flagella by *Babesia* at any stage in its life history. Dennis (1930) pointed out that *B. bigemina* is flagellate-like in its method of binary fission as well as in the possession of a blepharo-plast and rhizoplast, but in the absence of a flagellated stage or the demonstration of sexual phenomena in the invertebrate host, more definite assignment has been contingent upon further investigation of the life cycle in the tick.

In view of the life-cycle of *Babesia bigemina* that has been described above, the organism must still be considered a sporozoan. The entire development of *Babesia bigemina,* however, follows a simple procedure which would place it among the less specialized, i.e., phylogenetically younger of the Sporozoa. Even the type of sexual reproduction exhibited is of a very primitive nature, for the production of iso-gametes occurs in *Chlamydomonas,* one of the more primitive Phyto-monadina, though sexual phenomena are unproved in other Masti-gophora. The presence in *Babesia* of features of both the Mastigophora and Sporozoa makes speculation interesting. At least the morphology and life-cycle of *Babesia* give a clue to the origin of the Haemocytozoa, and provide a beautiful hypothetical "transitional" form between the haemoflagellates on one hand and the more specialized Haemosporidia on the other.

SUMMARY

The life-history and anatomy of *Margaropus annulatus* are reviewed, and an outline of the embryology is presented. From this description it is apparent that *M. annulatus* is ideally designed for its function as the biological vector of *Babesia bigemina.* Its suit-ability may be summarized as follows:

(1) The protozoan parasites are limited to the circulatory system of the bovine host, and the tick feeds on nothing but the blood of the host.

(2) The period of feeding of *M. annulatus* is long and since all of it is spent on a single animal the opportunity for taking in the *Babesia* is greatly enhanced, even though the host is but a "carrier" and the parasites are scarce in the peripheral blood.

(3) The gut of the tick is blind so that any parasites ingested and not lysed by the digestive ferments are retained in the gut and tend to accumulate, thus increasing the opportunity for gametes to become associated.

(4) The fact that *M. annulatus* normally attaches to but one host during its lifetime makes it obligatory that the parasites be passed on through the agency of the offspring.

(5) The extremely intimate relationship of the digestive tract and the reproductive organs makes it almost a foregone conclusion that any parasites leaving the gut and entering other tissues will invade the latter and come to occupy the ova.

(6) As has been shown, certain stages of *Babesia* migrate through-out the tissues of the developing tick, and since much of the embryonic

cell mass contributes to the formation of the salivary glands, it is almost inevitable that some of the parasites should come to lie in these structures, whence they may be transferred to a new host during the feeding processes of the seed tick.

The life-cycle of *Babesia bigemina* has two distinct phases: (*a*) an asexual cycle in the vertebrate host where multiplication takes place in the red blood corpuscles by binary fission; and (*b*) a simple sexual cycle in the tick.

When blood which is infected with *B. bigemina* is taken into the gut of the tick, many of the intracorpuscular parasites are soon freed. Certain of these normal-appearing parasites become transformed into gametes through growth and slight structural modification. The gametes are motile vermicule-like bodies which show no differentiation between the sexes. The gametes become associated in pairs, the individuals of which eventually fuse to form the zygote. The zygote becomes a motile oökinete which passes through the thin wall of the gut and penetrates the contiguous reproductive organs. The ova of the tick are invaded by the oökinetes which round up and grow to form sporonts. The sporont secretes a cyst within which it divides to form naked sporoblasts. The sporoblasts form multinucleate sporokinetes which migrate, and are carried by cell proliferation, throughout the tissues of the developing tick; some of the sporokinetes come to occupy the anlagen of the salivary glands. The sporokinete undergoes fragmentation to form the minute infectious sporozoites.

LITERATURE CITED

ALLEN, W. E.
  1905. Internal morphology of the American cattle tick. Trans. Am. Micr. Soc., **26**:245–280, 4 pls.

BABES, V.
  1888. Sur l'hémoglobinurie bacterienne du boeuf. C. R. Acad. Sci., Paris, **107**:692.

BETTENCOURT, A., FRANÇA, C., and BORGES, I.
  1907. Piroplasmose chez le daim. Arq. R. Inst. Bact. Camara Pestana, **7**:341.

BONNET, AMÉDÉE
  1907. Recherches sur l'anatomiee comparée et le dévelopment des ixodids. Ann. de l'Université de Lyon, **20**:1–185, 6 pls., 104 figs. in text.

BREINL, A., and HINDLE, E.
  1908. Contributions to the morphology and life history of *Piroplasma canis*. Ann. Trop. Med. and Parasitol., **2**:233–248, pls. 6–9.

CHRISTOPHERS, S. R.
  1906. The anatomy and histology of ticks. Sci. Mem. Med. San. Dept., Govt. of India, n.s., **23**:1–55, 6 pls., 8 figs. in text.
  1906a. Preliminary note on the development of *Piroplasma canis* in the tick. Brit. Med. Jour., Jan. 12, 1907, pp. 76–78, 1 fig. in text.
  1907b. *Piroplasma canis* and its life cycle in the tick. Sci. Mem. Med. San. Dept., Govt. of India, n.s., **29**:1–83, 3 pls.

COTTON, E. C.
  1908. Tick eradication. Bull. Agr. Exp. Sta. Univ. Tenn., **81**:55–71, 7 figs. and 3 tables in text.
  1915. The North American fever tick (*Boöphilus annulatus* Say). Notes on the life history. *Ibid.*, **113**:31–77, 13 tables and 15 figs. in text.

CRAWLEY, H.
  1915. Stage of *Piroplasma bigemina* in *Margaropus annulatus*. Jour. of Parasitol., **2**:87–90, 1 fig. in text.

CURTICE, COOPER
  1891. The biology of the cattle tick. Jour. Comp. Med. and Vet. Arch., **12**:113–319.
  1892. The cattle tick. Bull. Texas Agr. Exp. Sta., **24**:237–252, 2 pls.
  1896. On the extermination of the cattle tick and the disease spread by it. Jour. Comp. Med. and Vet. Arch., **17**:649–655.

DENNIS, E. W.
  1930. Morphology and binary fission of *Babesia bigemina* of Texas cattle fever. Univ. Calif. Publ. Zool., **33**:179–192, pls. 17, 18.

DONATIEN, A., and LESTOQUARD, F.
  1930. De la classification des piroplasmes des animaux domestique. Rev. Med. Vet. Exot., **3**:5–20, 2 figs. in text.

DSCHUNKOWSKY, E., and LUHS, J.
  1909. Entwickelungsformen von Piroplasmen in Zecken. Proc. 9th. Cong. Internat. Med. Vet., La Haye. Reprint, 6–8, 16, 17, and 21, 1 pl.

Du Toit, P. J.
  1918. Zur Systematik der Piroplasmen. Arch. f. Prot., 39:84–97.

Eastham, L. E. S.
  1930. The formation of germ layers in insects. Biol. Rev. 5:1–29, 2 figs.
    and 1 table in text.

Hunter, W. D., and Hooker, W. A.
  1907. The North American fever tick with notes on other species. Bull.
    U. S. Dept. Agr., Bur. of Entomology, 72:1–87, 4 pls. and 13 figs.
    in text.

Kleine, F. K.
  1906. Kultivierungsversuch der Hundepiroplasmen. Zeitschr. f. Hyg. u.
    Infectionskrankheit, 54:10–16, 2 pls.

Knuth, P., and Richters, E.
  1913. Über die Vermehrung von *Piroplasma canis in vitro.* Ber. Tierärzt.
    Wochenschr., 29:211–212.

Koch, R.
  1906. Entwickelungsgeschichte der Piroplasmen. Zeitschr. f. Hyg., 54:1–7,
    pls. 1–3.

Miller, W. W.
  1908. *Hepatozoon perniciosum* (n. gen., n. sp.); a haemogregarine patho-
    genic for white rats; with a description of the sexual cycle in the
    mite. Bull. Hyg. Lab., U. S. Pub. Health and Marine Hospital
    Service, Washington, 46:1–48, 20 pls.

Martini, E.
  1909. Entwickelung eines Rinderpiroplasmus. Zeitsch. f. Hyg., 64:285–390.

Nuttall, A. H. F., and Graham-Smith, B. S.
  1908. Multiplication of *Piroplasma bovis* with *P. pitheci* in the blood com-
    pared with that of *P. canis*, with notes on other species of *Piroplasma*.
    Parasitol., 1:134–142, pl. 11, and diagrams 1–4.
  1908a. The development of *Piroplasma canis* in culture. *Ibid.*, 1:243–260, 1 pl.

Patton, W. H.
  1895. The name of the southern or splenic cattle-fever parasite. Am.
    Naturalist, 29:498–501.

Reichenow, E.
  1921. Die Haemococcidien der Eidechsen Vorbemerkungen und I. Theil. Die
    Entwickelungsgeschichte von *Karyolysus*. Arch. f. Prot., Jena, 42:
    179–291, pls. 6–8.

Salmon, D. E., and Stiles, C. W.
  1901. The cattle ticks (Ixodoidea) of the United States. U. S. Dept. Agr.,
    Bur. Animal Ind., Ann. Rept., 17:380–491, pls. 74–98, figs. 47–238.

Say, Thomas
  1821. An account of the Arachnides of the United States. Jour. Acad.
    Nat. Sci., 2:59–83; Leconte ed., 2:9–24.

Schaudinn, F.
  1904. Generations und Wirtswechsel bei *Trypanosoma* und *Spirochaete*. Arb.
    a. d. Kaiserl. Gesundkeitsamts, 20:387–439, 20 figs. in text.

Schilling, C., and Meyer, K. F.
  1927. ''Piroplasmosen'' *in* Kolle u. Wassermann, Handb. d. pathog. Mikro-
    organismen (ed. 3; Fischer, Jena), 8:1–88, 34 figs. in text and
    pls. 1–4.

STARCOVICI, C.
  1893. Bermerkungen über den durch Babes entdeckten Blutparasiten und
        die durch denselben hervorgebrachten Krankheiten, die seuchen-
        hafte Hämoglobinurie des Rindes (Babes), das Texas-fieber (TH.
        Smith) und der Carceag der Schafe (Babes). Centralbl. Bakt.
        14:1–8.

SMITH, T., and KILBOURNE, F. H.
  1893. Investigations into the nature, causation, and prevention of Texas
        or southern cattle-fever. Bull. Bur. Animal Ind., U. S. Dept. Agr.,
        Washington, 1:177–304, 10 pls.

THOMPSON, J. G., and FANTHAM, H. B.
  1913. Culture of *Babesia canis* in vitro. Ann. Trop. Med., 7:621.

WAGNER, J.
  1894. Die Embryonalentwicklung von *Ixodes calcaratus*. Trudui St. Peterb.
        Obshch., 24:1–246; also in Bir. Arb. Zool. Lab., St. Petersburg,
        1894, pp. 1–246. Illus.

WENYON, C. M.
  1926. Protozoology (New York, Wm. Wood and Co.), 2:779–1563, 227 figs.
        in text.

WILLIAMS, S. R.
  1905. Anatomy of *Boöphilus annulatus* Say. Proc. Boston Soc. Nat. Hist.,
        32:313–334, pls. 18–22, 3 figs.

ZIEMANN, H.
  1913. Kulture der Malariaparasiten und Piroplasmen in vitro. Arch. f.
        Schiffs u. Trop. Hyg., 17:361–391, pls. 6 and 7.

EXPLANATION OF PLATES

All figures drawn with the aid of a camera lucida.

PLATE 23

Fig 1. Median sagittal section through a mature ovum of *Margaropus annulatus*, showing the disposition of yolk and the germinal vesicle. Iron-haematoxylin stain × 130.

Fig. 2. Median sagittal section showing blastoderm and the proliferation of the endodermal ridge; anterior region is to the left. Iron-haematoxylin stain × 56.

Fig. 3. Sagittal section showing the proliferation of the anterior ectodermal cell mass. Iron-haematoxylin × 56.

Fig. 4. Transverse section through the fourth pair of limb-buds, showing the distribution of the mesoderm, and the endodermal ridge. Iron-haematoxylin × 56.

Fig. 5. Left half of transverse section through the anterior region of a newly-hatched tick larva, showing the relation of the salivary gland anlagen to the brain mass; also the sparse distribution of the endoderm just dorsal to these structures. Iron-haematoxylin stain × 56.

Fig. 6. Median sagittal section through an embryo just previous to hatching. Shows the relationship of the digestive tract to the brain, the appearance of the excretory vesicle, and the dorso-ventral muscles; the gut has not formed. Delafield's stain × 130.

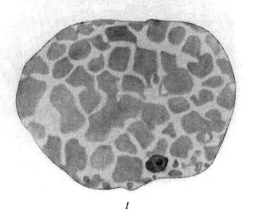

1

2

3

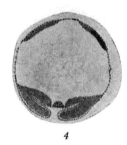

4

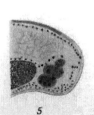

5

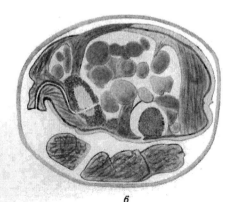

6

PLATE 24

Figs. 7, 8, and 9.   Trophozoites of *Babesia bigemina* in red blood cells of the bovine host.   Giemsa's stain × 4360.

Figs. 10, 11, and 12.   *B. bigemina* stained with iron-haematoxylin × 4360.

Fig. 10.   Small sporozoite i.e., young trophozoite, in a red blood cell.

Fig. 11.   Two small *B. bigemina*, probably resulting from the division of such a form as the one in fig. 10.

Fig. 12.   Two large trophozoites of *B. bigemina* showing structure of the nucleus, and the blepharoplast and rhizoplast.

Figs. 13–18.   *Babesia bigemina*, trophozoites, as they appear in the gut of the tick.   Iron-haematoxylin × 2562.

Figs. 19–20.   Transformation of trophozoites into the isogametes.   Iron-haematoxylin × 2562.

Fig. 21.   Typical vermicule-like isogamete.   Iron-haematoxylin × 2562.

Figs. 22–24.   Herpetomonad-like nonflagellated forms seen in the gut of the tick.   Iron-haematoxylin × 2562.

Figs. 25–26.   Larger forms seen in the gut, showing an apical chromatin granule and traces of a fibril.   Iron-haematoxylin × 2562.

Figs. 27–29.   Club-shaped bodies of *B. canis*.   Interpreted by Christophers as dividing forms.   Redrawn from Christophers (1907) for comparison.   Giemsa's stain × 1000 (?).

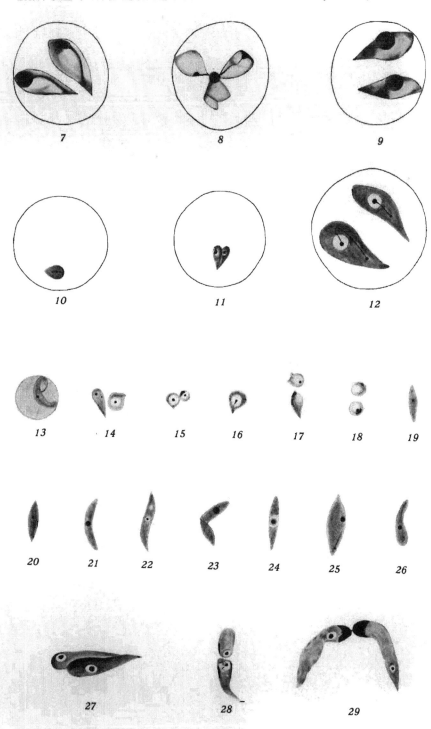

PLATE 25

All figures except fig. 32 stained with iron-haematoxylin ×2562.

Fig. 30. Two specimens of *Babesia bigemina,* typical of the forms most common in the gut of the tick.

Fig. 31. Associated isogametes. Beginning of syngamy.

Fig. 32. Associated gametes observed in a fresh smear of the contents of the gut of the tick.

Figs. 33–34. Later stage of syngamy, seen in stained smear of contents of the gut.

Figs. 35–36. Oökinetes of *B. bigemina* in the gut of the tick.

Fig. 37. One of a large number of oökinetes in a section of a mature tick ovum.

Fig. 38. Large oökinete showing an anterior cup. From a smear of tick ova.

Fig. 39. Parasites of unknown relationship observed in smear of tick ova.

Fig. 40. Part of an oökinete in a section of an ovum of the tick.

Fig. 41. Two oökinetes in a large embryonic cell of a nymph.

Fig. 42. Oökinete in section of ovum of tick.

Fig. 43. Sporont imbedded in the yolk of ovum of tick.

Fig. 44. Increase in number of nuclei in a small sporocyst in the yolk of ovum of tick.

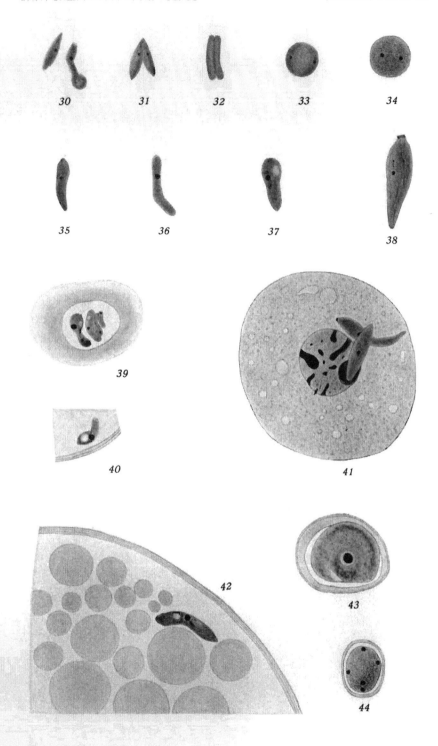

PLATE 26

Fig. 45.   Sporoblasts of *B. bigemina* from smear of early embryonic stage of the tick.   Iron-haematoxylin × 4360.

Fig. 46.   Sporoblasts in section of tick ovum.   Iron-haematoxylin × 4360.

Fig. 47.   Sporokinetes in a smear of heavily parasitized tissue of tick larva, showing characteristic shapes.   Iron-haematoxylin × 4360.

Fig. 48.   Large and rather atypical *B. bigemina* as seen in a single focal plane of a heavily infected salivary acinus of a nymph.   Delafield's haematoxylin × 2562.

Fig. 49.   Typical sporozoites of *B. bigemina* as seen in a single focal plane of a heavily infected portion of a salivary anlage of the tick.   Delafield's haematoxylin × 4360.

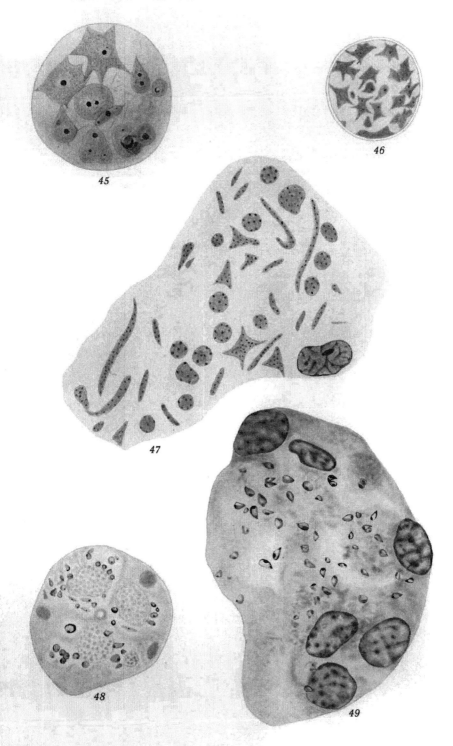

45

46

47

48

49

PLATE 27

Fig. 50. Heavily parasitized salivary gland tissue as seen in a squash preparation of a seed tick, stained with Giemsa. The stippled appearance of the lobe to the right is due to the nuclei of the sporozoites which are so numerous that the outlines of the individuals are seldom distinguishable × 500.

Fig. 51. Sporozoites of *B. bigemina* in the sheath of a muscle fiber of a tick larva. Giemsa × 1281.

Fig. 52. The right end of a transverse section of a heavily parasitized seed tick, showing the distribution of *Babesia* in the cells of the anlage of a gut diverticulum, in the blastoderm, and in the sheath of the dorso-ventral muscles. Salivary tissue heavily stained; cuticle of the tick is not shown. Delafield's haematoxylin × 1083.

Fig. 53. A lobe of embryonic salivary gland, heavily parasitized with sporokinetes of *B. bigemina*. Squash preparation; iron-haematoxylin × 800.

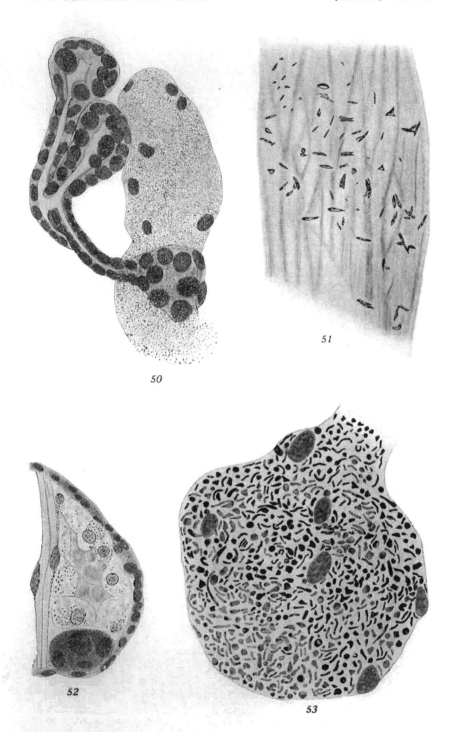

50

51

52

53

PLATE 28

A schematic diagram of the life-cycle of *B. bigemina*.

Figs. 1–6. The cycle of *B. bigemina* in the blood of the bovine host, showing the method of binary fission.

Fig. 7. *B. bigemina* which have just been taken into the gut of the tick.

Fig. 8. Trophozoites of *B. bigemina* which have been freed in the gut of the tick.

Fig. 9. The vermicule-like isogametes.

Fig. 10. Beginning of syngamy. Association of the gametes in pairs.

Fig. 11. Completion of syngamy.

Fig. 12. The motile zygote, or oökinete.

Figs. 13 and 14. The oökinete passes through the wall of the gut of the tick, through the oviduct, and enters the ovum.

Fig. 15. The sporont formed by the rounding-up and growth of the oökinete.

Figs. 16 and 17. Formation of sporoblasts.

Fig. 18. Sporokinetes in one of the large cells which are destined to form part of a salivary acinus.

Fig. 19. Sporozoites, formed by the fragmentation of sporokinetes, in the salivary gland (a single acinus shown) of the larva of the tick, whence they are transferred into the blood of a new host.

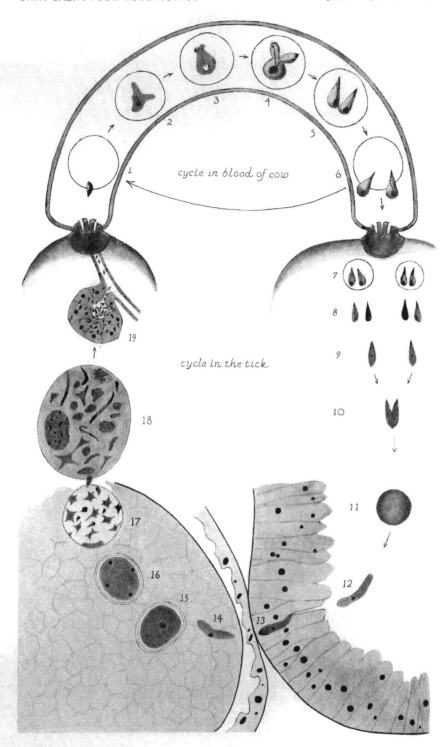

cycle in blood of cow

cycle in the tick